COOL
Sets & Props

How to Stage
Your Very Own Show

Karen Latchana Kenney

Consulting Editor, Diane Craig, M.A./Reading Specialist

ABDO
Publishing Company

Visit us at www.abdopublishing.com

Published by ABDO Publishing Company,
8000 West 78th Street, Edina, Minnesota 55439.
Copyright © 2010 by Abdo Consulting Group, Inc.
International copyrights reserved in all countries. No part
of this book may be reproduced in any form without written
permission from the publisher. The Checkerboard Library™
is a trademark and logo of ABDO Publishing Company.

Printed in the United States.
Design and Production: Colleen Dolphin, Mighty Media, Inc.
Photo Credits: Colleen Dolphin, Shutterstock,
iStockphoto (Zsolt Biczó, Pilar Echeverria, Michal Koziarski)
Series Editor: Katherine Hengel, Pam Price
Activity Production: Britney Haeg

The following manufacturers/names appearing in this book are
trademarks: Crayola® Washable Glitter Glue, Elmer's® Glue-All™,
Office Depot® Posterboard, Scotch® Magic Tape™ and
Target® Aluminum Foil

Library of Congress Cataloging-in-Publication Data

Kenney, Karen Latchana.
  Cool sets & props : how to stage your very own show /
Karen Latchana Kenney.
     p. cm. -- (Cool performances)
  Includes webliography and index.
  ISBN 978-1-60453-718-5
  1. Theaters--Stage-setting and scenery--Juvenile literature. I.
Title. II. Title: Cool sets and props.

PN2091.S8K385 2010
792.02'5--dc22
                                              2009000408

Note to Adult Helpers

To complete the activities in this
book, kids will need some supervision,
especially when they are using utility
knives and ladders. Remind kids that
they need an adult to help them
with these activities. Likewise, if kids
are scrounging around for materials,
remind them to get permission from an
adult before they use anything.

Before beginning, find a good place
for kids to work. Make sure there is
a specific cutting area with padding
underneath. Protect surfaces with
newspaper or an old sheet. When
painting, find a space that is well
ventilated and make sure kids protect
their clothing.

Get the Picture!

There are many activities and how-to photos
in this title. Each how-to photo has a color
border around it, so match the border color
to the appropriate activity step!

 activity step →

Contents

CREATING COOL PERFORMANCES

Imagine putting on your very own show! Performing in front of an audience sounds fun, right? It is! You can pretend to be anything you want to be. Create an **illusion** through your costume, makeup, and stage. Tell a story by acting out a script. Put everything together, and you have a cool show!

You can create many kinds of shows. You can tell a funny story or a serious story. Put on a musical or a fairy tale. Creep out your audience with a monster or a ghost story. You can even be an alien on a strange planet!

Cool Performances Series

Cool Costumes	Cool Scripts & Acting
Cool Makeup	Cool Sets & Props
Cool Productions	Cool Special Effects

Permission

Before beginning, find out if you have permission to put on a show. Making the set pieces and props in this book will require cutting, painting, and hanging. Get permission before cutting or painting anything.

Safety

Make sure your work space has a window or door you can open for fresh air. This is important if you are using paint. Protect the floor by laying down some newspaper or an old sheet. Find an adult to help you if you need to use a utility knife or ladder. Also, wear utility gloves and an old shirt to protect your clothes and hands from paint.

Clean Up

Remember to clean up after finishing your set pieces and props! Put all your tools and materials away. Place lids on open containers. Wipe down the surfaces you worked on. Throw away unusable scraps. And remember to store your finished set pieces and props in an appropriate area.

Show Styles

There are many show styles. Shows can be one style or a combination of styles. Here are just a few.

Drama

Emotions are important in a drama. A dramatic show might be sad or it could make audiences laugh!

Fairy Tale

Fairy tales teach lessons. They have make-believe characters such as fairies, unicorns, and goblins.

Fantasy

Imaginary creatures make this kind of show fantastic! Mad scientists create monsters in laboratories, and aliens fly through space!

Musical

Singing is just as important as acting in a musical. Songs tell parts of the story.

SETTING THE STAGE

How a scene is created

It all starts with an empty stage. For each show, a new and interesting set is created. A set helps the audience learn about the characters, their lives, and the story. Sets create physical backgrounds for the acting in a show.

Sets usually include backdrops, props, and set pieces. A backdrop is a painted **mural** that hangs at the back of the stage. It shows things that are too difficult to make, or things that are supposed to be really big or far away. A prop, which is short for property, is a thing that actors can hold and move around the stage. A set piece is a larger object that stays still on stage. Pieces of furniture or castle towers can be set pieces.

When you make a set, it has to fit the story! In professional shows, set designers carefully study the script and decide how the stage should look. They also work with directors to make sure the set fits their **vision** for the show.

When making your set, think about your script. This will help you decide what to put on your set. For example, what time of year is it? Does your show take place in the future or in the past? Styles change with time, so make sure your set looks right!

There are many set pieces and props that you can make at home. Using simple materials and your imagination, you can create cool backgrounds for any show. Create a fairy tale castle or a pirate ship. Just imagine it and get to work. You have a set to build!

prop

backdrop

set piece

FOUND & BOUGHT

Preparing to create cool sets

Creating the set for your show is easy! You can find many props and set pieces in your home. An old chair can become a king's throne. An old phone can be a great prop. Look around and see what you can find, but always ask for permission first!

You should also ask for permission to spend money on materials. Find out how much you can spend. This will be the budget for your production. Garage sales and thrift stores are great places to shop.

Whatever you can't find, you can make! A few common items such as a utility knife, glue, and cardboard will help you create a great set. The activities in this book will give you a great start.

STAGE KIT

To complete the activities in this book, you will need these basic materials.

cardboard boxes

tissue paper

old flat sheets

tablecloth

banner paper

stool

poster board

markers

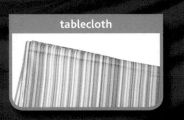

glitter glue

plastic stemware

ruler

dowel or stick

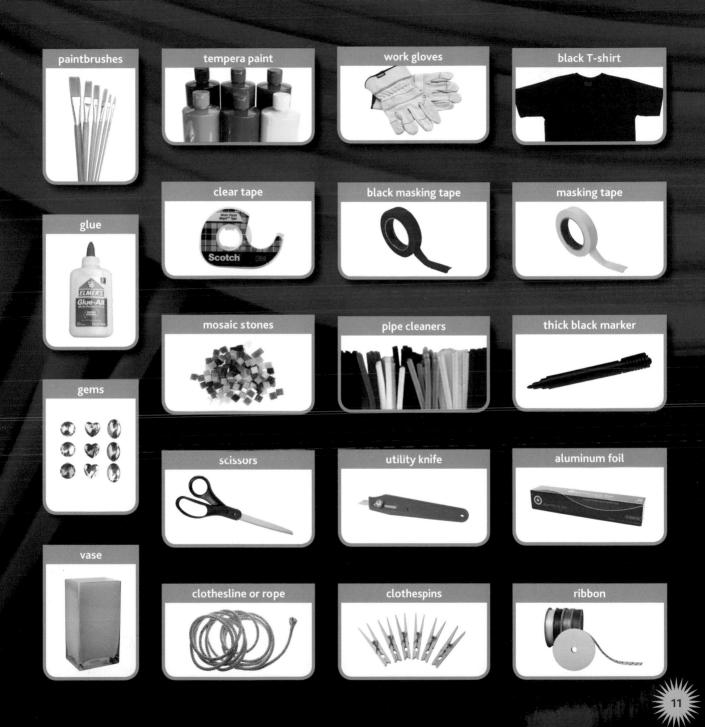

paintbrushes

tempera paint

work gloves

black T-shirt

glue

clear tape

black masking tape

masking tape

gems

mosaic stones

pipe cleaners

thick black marker

scissors

utility knife

aluminum foil

vase

clothesline or rope

clothespins

ribbon

Believable Backdrops

If you want a cool background, paint a backdrop! Backdrops are painted **murals** that hang at the back of the stage. They show large scenery. You can change them quickly and easily if the play has more than one **setting**.

STAGE KIT

- paper, 8.5 x 11 inches (21.6 x 27.9 cm)
- pencil
- banner paper
- scissors
- thick black marker
- gloves and an old shirt
- tempera paint
- paintbrushes
- masking tape

1 Decide what kinds of backdrops will match your story. You might want to make different backdrops for different scenes. Check out "Set the Scene" on page 15 for backdrop ideas.

2 Sketch out your scene on a piece of paper.

Get Into Perspective!

It's easy to show depth and distance in your backdrops. To make something look like it is far way, draw it at the top of your backdrop and make it small. To make something look like it is close, draw it towards the bottom of your backdrop and make it really big.

3 Decide how big you want your backdrop to be. Try cutting out two pieces of banner paper that are each 8 × 2 feet (2.4 × .6 m). Tape these two pieces together for a backdrop that is 8 × 4 feet (2.4 × 1.2 m).

13

Using your sketch as a guide, draw your scene onto your backdrop with a pencil. Take your time and step back often to see how things look from a distance. When you are happy with your sketch, trace over your pencil marks with a thick black marker.

It's time to paint! Make sure there is fresh air in your work space. Wear gloves and an old shirt. Use wide paintbrushes for large areas. Use fine paintbrushes for the details. Let your backdrop dry for several hours, and then touch up your outlines with your thick black marker.

Roll up pieces of tape and put them on the back of your backdrop. Attach your backdrop to the wall.

Set the Scene

Try combining these elements to make cool backdrops.

Alien Landscape

rocky land, planets in the sky, purple trees, orange streams

Robot Workshop

computer keyboards, electronic parts, springs and screws, tables, tools

Witch's Kitchen

black **cauldron**, large fireplace, strange ingredients hanging from the ceiling, cobwebs, spiders

Creepy Cemetery

night sky, sliver moon, gravestones with scary names, skeleton hand coming out of the ground, bats

Fairy Tale Fantasy

castle in the distance, green fields, unicorn or horse

Royal Feast

two thrones, stone walls, **tapestry**

An Animal's View

big mouse hole in the wall, the legs of a really large table, human feet and legs under the table

Cloth Backdrops

You can make backdrops out of old flat sheets! Hang a clothesline across your stage. Make sure you attach the ends of your clothesline to something secure, such as hooks. Then use clothespins to attach your cloth backdrop to the clothesline. This method works great for shows that are staged in garages!

Big Bushes

Bring the outdoors on stage! These cardboard bushes are easy to move around your set. Find some old boxes to get started!

STAGE KIT

- cardboard, at least 4 x 3 feet (1.2 x .9 m)
- pencil
- work gloves and old shirt
- tempera paint
- paintbrushes
- markers
- utility knife
- ruler
- cardboard, 3 x 3 feet (.9 m x .9 m)
- masking tape

SAFETY CHECK!

- Do you have permission to use a utility knife? Ask an adult to help you.

- Before you start cutting, it is a good idea to place an extra piece of cardboard underneath the piece you are cutting. This should protect your work space.

1 Using a pencil, draw a bush on the larger piece of cardboard. Try making rounded or spiky edges.

2 It's time to add some color! Make sure there is fresh air in your work space. Put on work gloves and an old shirt. Paint the entire front side of the bush green.

3 When the paint is dry, use markers to add leaves and twigs. Ask an adult to help you cut out the bush.

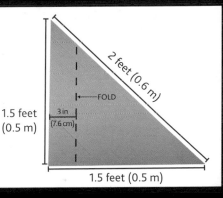

1.5 feet (0.5 m)   3 in (7.6 cm)   FOLD   2 feet (0.6 m)

1.5 feet (0.5 m)

4 For the stand, draw a triangle on the smaller piece of cardboard as shown. Two sides of the triangle should be 1.5 feet (0.5 m) long. The third side should be two feet (0.6 m) long. Ask an adult to help you cut out the stand. Use a ruler to make a mark that is 3 inches (7.6 cm) from the left side of the triangle. Draw a faint vertical line over your mark. Fold your cardboard along this vertical line. This is the stand for the bush.

5 Use masking tape to secure the folded section of the stand to the back of the bush. Make sure the bottom of the stand lines up with the bottom of the bush.

Magical Mirror

This fun mirror is easy to make and works on stage! Real mirrors are glass with a metal coating on one side. They are heavy and hard to work with during a performance. This mirror uses aluminum foil instead.

STAGE KIT
- 2 pieces of cardboard, 18 x 24 inches (46 x 61 cm) each
- utility knife
- pencil
- ruler
- aluminum foil
- glue
- work gloves and an old shirt
- tempera paint
- paintbrushes
- gems
- mosaic stones
- glitter glue

1. Ask an adult to help you cut out two pieces of cardboard that are each 18 x 24 inches (46 x 61 cm). One piece will be the back of the mirror, and the other will be the frame.

2. Draw a rectangle in the middle of one of the pieces of cardboard. The rectangle should be 16 x 12 inches (41 x 56 cm). Ask an adult to help you cut it out with a utility knife. Discard the rectangle. Now you have a frame!

3. Lay the frame on the mirror back. Trace the frame opening onto the mirror back.

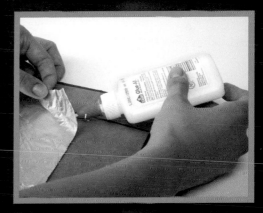

4. Glue aluminum foil onto the mirror back. Make sure it slightly overlaps the rectangle you traced in step 3. This is the glass part of the mirror.

5. Paint the frame. Make sure there is fresh air in your work space. Wear gloves and an old shirt. When the paint is dry, decorate your frame with gems, mosaic stones, and glitter glue. Glue the frame onto the mirror back.

Cool Boxes

A cardboard box can easily become a castle tower or a rocket ship! A castle tower is great for fairy tales or historical dramas set in **medieval** times. Rocket ships are great for shows set in the future or outer space!

STAGE KIT
- large cardboard boxes
- ruler
- pencil
- utility knife
- work gloves and an old shirt
- tempera paints
- paintbrushes
- thick black marker
- 2 black pipe cleaners
- gems
- tablecloth
- vase

1. Find a rectangular box that is 1 foot (30.5 cm) taller than you are.

2. Stand in front of the box. Draw a window at eye level.

3. Ask an adult to help you cut out the window using a utility knife.

4. Draw a **design** on the box with a pencil. Make sure the window is in the design. Draw bricks on the tower and put **crenellations** at the very top.

crenellations

5. Paint the design. Make sure there is fresh air in your work space. Wear gloves and an old shirt. Try painting a blue sky behind the castle tower. Let the box dry, then use a thick black marker to outline the design.

CASTLE TOWER

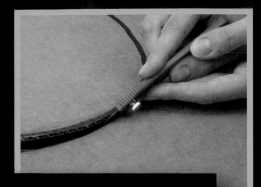

ROCKET SHIP

1 Find a rectangular box that is 1 foot (30.5 cm) taller than you are.

2 Stand in front of the box. Draw a circular window at eye level.

3 Ask an adult to help you cut out the window using a utility knife.

4 Draw a rocket ship on the box with a pencil. Make sure the window is in the design. Draw an oval shape with a point at the top. Make the bottom of the rocket ship flat. Add some flames!

5 Paint the **design**. Make sure there is fresh air in your work space. Wear gloves and an old shirt. Try painting a starry night behind the rocket ship. Let the box dry, then use a thick black marker to outline the design.

Cardboard Creations

PAINT A GRAY SQUARE WITH A BLACK BORDER ON THE FRONT OF THE BOX. DRAW SOME GRAY BUTTONS ALONG THE BOTTOM. TO MAKE ANTENNAE, ATTACH TWO BLACK PIPE CLEANERS TO THE TOP.

PUT A TABLECLOTH OVER A BOX. ADD A VASE!

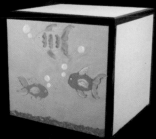

PAINT ONE SIDE OF THE BOX BLUE. DRAW TROPICAL FISH SWIMMING AROUND.

PAINT A BOX SO THAT IT LOOKS LIKE A TREASURE CHEST. ADD SOME GEMS TO MAKE IT LOOK FANCY!

Set the Scene

Try combining these elements to make cool sets.

Alien Landscape

rocket ships, purple bushes

Exotic Island

brown blanket for sand, seashells, cardboard waves

Medieval Castle

long table with chairs, golden goblets, cardboard chandelier

Magical Forest

bushes, trees, paper leaves on the ground, a path cut from cardboard on the stage

Pirate Ship

wooden steering wheel, benches, treasure chest

Bustling City

skyscrapers, car cut out of cardboard, bus stop sign

Golden Goblet

Turn plastic into gold! A goblet is a fancy drinking glass with a stem and a base. Use goblets when your script calls for royal dinners or magic potions.

1 Paint the plastic **stemware** with gold tempera paint. Make sure there is fresh air in your work space. Let it dry completely.

2 Glue gems along the top edge of the glass. If you like, add some to the base of the glass too.

3 Add fancy **designs** with glitter glue. Try adding a wavy line around the middle of the glass. Or write your initial.

STAGE KIT
- plastic stemware
- gold tempera paint
- paintbrush
- work gloves and old shirt
- gems
- glue
- glitter glue

MagicWand

1 Draw a five-point star on a piece of poster board. Cut it out with a pair of scissors. Make a second star that is exactly the same size.

Enchant your audience with this wand! It's perfect for a magician, fairy, witch, or wizard. Just give it a wave and make your show magical.

2 Tape pieces of ribbon to the middle of one star. Secure the dowel to the middle of the star using masking tape.

STAGE KIT

- poster board
- pencil
- scissors
- ribbon
- dowel or stick about two feet (0.6 m) long
- masking tape
- glue
- markers
- glitter glue
- gems

3 Put a line of glue around the outer edge of the star. Press the other star on top. Line it up so that the points of the stars match. Hold the stars together until the glue dries.

4 Now decorate your wand! Add some gems or glitter glue for some sparkle. Presto!

Beautiful Bouquet

Make colorful flowers from tissue paper! A bouquet can be used on stage in many different ways. For example, in Victorian times, ladies carried small bouquets called nosegays. They held the flowers to their noses to hide bad smells.

1 Cut out 10 squares of tissue paper. The squares should be 4 × 4 inches (10 × 10 cm). Get creative with the colors you choose!

2 Stack the 10 squares of tissue paper together. Fold the stack in half. Then fold it in half again.

3 Cut a petal shape out of your stack as shown. Don't cut the folded edge! This is the middle of your flower. Unfold the paper and then use a pencil to poke a hole through the middle of your petals.

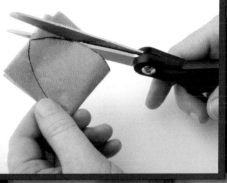

4 Push a green pipe cleaner through the hole. This is your stem! Leave about two inches (5 cm) of pipe cleaner on one side. Bend that section into a small ball. This is the center of your flower.

5 Spread out the petals of your flower. Make as many flowers as you want. Tie them together with the ribbon to make a bouquet. Beautiful!

Shiny Sword

Fight battles on stage using this sword! Make a sword fit for a knight. Or make a pirate's cutlass, which is a curved sword. Either way, your audience will be impressed!

STAGE KIT
- cardboard, at least 2 x 24 inches (5 x 61 cm)
- pencil
- utility knife
- ruler
- 2 cardboard rectangles, 2 x 6 inches (5 x 15 cm) each
- black masking tape
- aluminum foil
- clear tape
- gems
- glitter glue

On the large piece of cardboard, draw a sword blade. Make it pointed at one end and square at the opposite end. Ask an adult to help you cut it out.

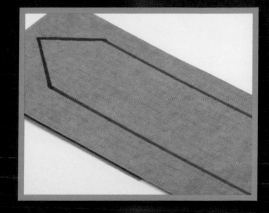

Use a pencil to make a small mark that is six inches (15 cm) from the square end of the blade. Put one of the cardboard rectangles at your mark. Put the second cardboard rectangle behind it on the other side of the blade. This is your sword's guard.

Cover the guard and grip with black masking tape.

Cover the blade with pieces of aluminum foil. Use clear tape to hold the foil in place. Decorate the **hilt** with gems or glitter glue.

Set the Scene

To make a scary pirate cutlass, draw a curved blade instead of a straight one. Glue gems on the hilt. Ahoy matey!

CONCLUSION

Now that you've made your backdrops, props, and set pieces, it's time to put it all together. Arrange everything on stage and step back to see how it looks. This is called stage **setting**. Whether it is a realistic scene or a fantasyland, the set you've imagined is now a reality.

But you need more than backdrops, sets, and props to put on a show. Check out the other books in the Cool Performances series to learn more about putting on a show. Learn how to use makeup and costumes to create different looks. Practice your acting skills and try writing a script. Add lighting and special effects. Promote your show with flyers and banners. Have fun and let your imagination run wild!

GLOSSARY

cauldron – a large kettle or pot.

crenellation – a notch in the top of a wall.

design – a sketch or an outline of something that you are going to make.

enchant – to charm or attract someone.

hilt – the grip and guard of a sword or dagger.

illusion – something that looks real but is not.

medieval – of or belonging to the Middle Ages (from AD 500 to 1500).

mural – a picture painted on a wall or a ceiling.

perspective – the art of giving objects drawn on a flat surface the illusion of being three-dimensional.

setting – the place where a story happens.

stemware – a glass with a thin stem and a flat base.

tapestry – a heavy woven fabric decorated with detailed designs or pictures.

vision – an idea formed in the imagination.

Web Sites

To learn more about putting on a show, visit ABDO Publishing Company on the World Wide Web at www.abdopublishing.com. Web sites about theater are featured on our Book Links page. These links are routinely monitored and updated to provide the most current information available.

INDEX